EXPLORE OUR WORLD

PHYSICAL SCIENCE

Cars Get Smart

MICHÈLE DUFRESNE

TABLE OF CONTENTS

How Do Driverless Cars Work?	2
Will We Be Safer?	10
Who Will Use a Self-Driving Car?	16
Glossary/Index	20

PIONEER VALLEY EDUCATIONAL PRESS, INC

HOW DO DRIVERLESS CARS WORK?

Imagine if you could ride to school or a friend's house in a car without an adult driving you! Imagine a car that is smart enough to drive itself.

Some people believe that, in the near future, there will be self-driving cars that can quickly pick up and drop off passengers.

Many companies are spending billions of dollars to develop **autonomous**, or self-driving, cars. Just like there was a race to be the first to the moon, automakers around the world are racing to be the first to create a safe self-driving car.

Airplanes have had automatic flight systems since the 1930s. Pilots still need to control the takeoff and landing, but most of the time the plane flies in **AUTOPILOT.**

Most modern cars have computers inside them. For example, turning the steering wheel does not actually turn the wheels. Instead, it sends a message to a computer system, and the computer helps to turn the wheels. Many newer cars use computers and cameras to sense what is nearby. They may beep or brake if they get too close to another car. Some cars can even have a wireless internet signal.

Three things are needed to turn a regular car into a self-driving vehicle. First, a self-driving car needs a **GPS**. A GPS uses satellites to figure out where the car is and where the driver wants to go. The GPS can also help avoid traffic jams and road construction.

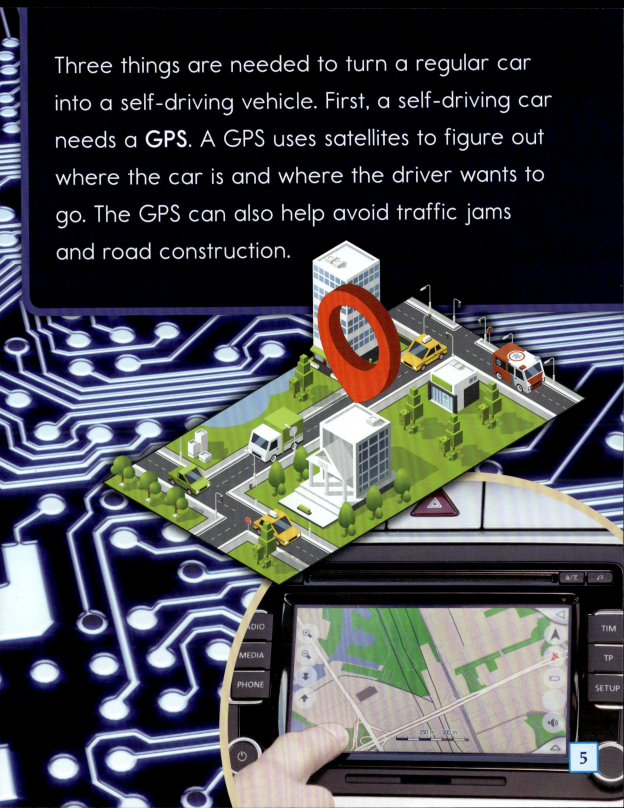

Second, a self-driving car needs a system that can recognize the conditions of the road. Is there snow or rain? Are there potholes to avoid? Is there a person walking across the road?

A person driving a car has to make many decisions to avoid obstacles or other cars in the road. Self-driving cars use **sensors** to make these decisions. The sensors are placed on all sides of the car and are often better than the human eye at understanding their surroundings. They can see clearly behind the car and respond more quickly than a person.

The third thing a driverless car needs is a system that can use the GPS and the conditions of the road to make decisions about what to do. Should the car stop or go? Should the car slow down or speed up?

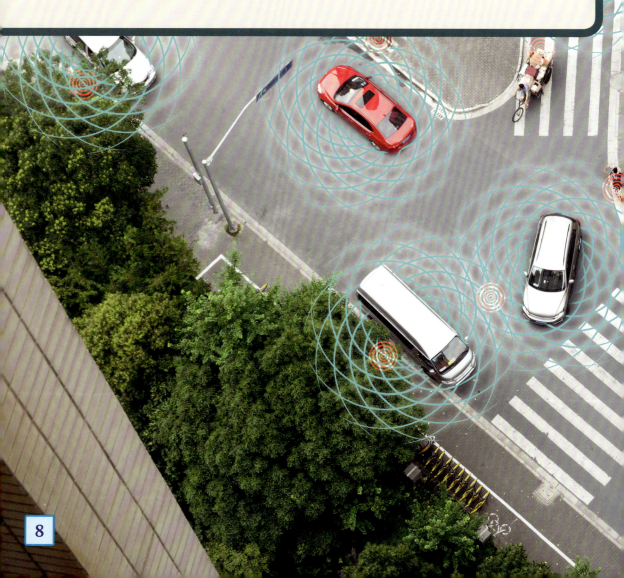

The driverless cars of the future may be able to actually talk to one another. They may talk to each other about where they are going and when they will be turning.

MORE TO EXPLORE

A driverless car not only needs sensors that can see, but it also needs **SENSORS THAT CAN HEAR.** That way, the car will hear when something like a fire truck is approaching and will get out of the way to let it pass.

WILL WE BE SAFER?

Sometimes drivers do not watch the road. Some people are texting a friend or changing the radio station instead of looking at the road. Millions of people around the world are killed or injured in car accidents each year.

The primary reason some people want driverless cars is the belief that they will make us safer. The driverless cars will not be distracted by a phone or a radio.

Modern cars are much safer than cars built long ago. New cars have special features that have helped save lives. Riding in cars has become much safer since people began to use seat belts and cars came with airbags. Fewer people have died in accidents.

It is possible that driverless cars will prevent terrible accidents that kill people in cars each day. Some researchers have an expectation that driverless cars could even prevent all car accidents.

At first there will be self-driving cars sharing the road with cars that are driven by people. Some researchers think this might make driving more dangerous.

But when all cars are self-driving, many researchers believe there will be fewer mistakes and fewer accidents.

There are already some driverless cars on the road, and a few of them have been involved in crashes. However, most of these were caused by mistakes made by the driver of another car. For example, some of the accidents were caused by humans not stopping at stoplights or rear-ending the self-driving car.

When you are driving, you have to make decisions to keep yourself and others safe. But sometimes neither decision seems good. What if a driverless car was faced with two bad choices? For example, if a person crossed the road in front of a driverless car, the car would have to swerve out of the way. But swerving may not always be a safe choice. There could be a bus with passengers in the other lane. What would the self-driving car decide to do? Would it make a better decision than a human?

WHO WILL USE A SELF-DRIVING CAR?

If cars could drive themselves, people who have trouble seeing could travel to the library or the grocery store without having to ask for help. People with **disabilities** could be more independent. But what would they do in an emergency if the car system failed? Should there always be another person with them who can take over if they need to? We will need to think about these kinds of questions as we make new laws for self-driving cars.

The latest **GOOGLE DRIVERLESS CAR** is a little two-seater with no steering wheel, no gas, and no brake pedal. The only driving you can do in these cars is done by typing instructions on a screen!

Even though self-driving cars may be much safer for travel, they are still a little frightening to think about. When people are asked if they want a self-driving car, many say no. Many people do not want to give up having a steering wheel or gas and brake pedals. A lot of people really like to drive.

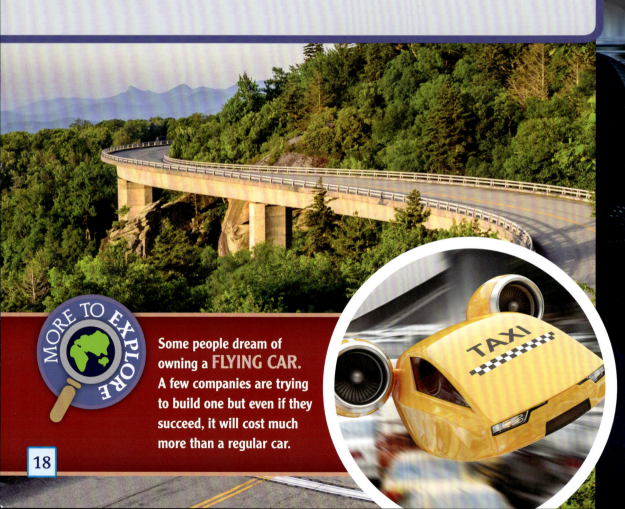

MORE TO EXPLORE

Some people dream of owning a **FLYING CAR**. A few companies are trying to build one but even if they succeed, it will cost much more than a regular car.

The idea that you could read a book or take a nap instead of focusing on the road and navigating traffic can be very appealing. As cars get smarter and help with more of the driving tasks, we may warm up to the idea of a car driving itself.

GLOSSARY

autonomous
existing or acting separately from other things or people

disabilities
illnesses or injuries that damage or limit a person's physical or mental abilities

GPS
Global Positioning System, a network of devices that use satellites to tell a person where they are

sensors
devices that detect heat, light, sound, or motion

INDEX

accidents 10–13
airbags 11
airplanes 3
automakers 3
automatic flight systems 3
autonomous 3
autopilot 3
brake 4, 17, 18
cameras 4
computers 4
decisions 7, 8, 14
disabilities 16
driverless 2, 8, 9, 10–11, 13, 14, 17
emergency 16
flying car 18
gas 17, 18
Google 17
GPS 5, 8
instructions 17
internet 4
mistakes 12–13
passengers 2, 14
pilots 3
radio 10
researchers 11, 12
satellites 5
seat belts 11
self-driving 2–3, 5–7, 12–14, 16, 18
sensors 7, 9
steering wheel 4, 17, 18
stoplights 13
systems 3, 4, 6, 8, 16
travel 16, 18